Today, I am gratef

Today, I am grateful for

Today, I am grateful for

....

....

....

....

....

....

....

....

....

....

....

....

....

....

....

....

....

....

....

....

....

....

....

....

Today, I am grateful for

Today, I am grateful for

Today, I am grateful for

Today, I am grateful for

....
....
....
....
....
....
....
....
....
....
....
....
....
....
....
....
....
....
....
....
....
....
....
....

Today, I am grateful for

Today, I am grateful for

....

....

....

....

....

....

....

....

....

....

....

....

....

....

....

....

....

....

....

....

....

....

....

....

Today, I am grateful for

Today, I am grateful for

Today, I am grateful for

Today, I am grateful for

....

....

....

....

....

....

....

....

....

....

....

....

....

....

....

....

....

....

....

....

....

....

....

....

Today, I am grateful for

....

....

....

....

....

....

....

....

....

....

....

....

....

....

....

....

....

....

....

....

....

....

....

....

Today, I am grateful for

....

....

....

....

....

....

....

....

....

....

....

....

....

....

....

....

....

....

....

....

....

....

....

....

Today, I am grateful for

Today, I am grateful for

....
....
....
....
....
....
....
....
....
....
....
....
....
....
....
....
....
....
....
....
....
....
....
....

Today, I am grateful for

Today, I am grateful for

Today, I am grateful for

Today, I am grateful for

Today, I am grateful for

Today, I am grateful for

Today, I am grateful for

Today, I am grateful for

Today, I am grateful for

……………………………………………………………………………………

……………………………………………………………………………………

……………………………………………………………………………………

……………………………………………………………………………………

……………………………………………………………………………………

……………………………………………………………………………………

……………………………………………………………………………………

……………………………………………………………………………………

……………………………………………………………………………………

……………………………………………………………………………………

……………………………………………………………………………………

……………………………………………………………………………………

……………………………………………………………………………………

……………………………………………………………………………………

……………………………………………………………………………………

……………………………………………………………………………………

……………………………………………………………………………………

……………………………………………………………………………………

……………………………………………………………………………………

……………………………………………………………………………………

……………………………………………………………………………………

……………………………………………………………………………………

……………………………………………………………………………………

……………………………………………………………………………………

Today, I am grateful for

Today, I am grateful for

Today, I am grateful for

....

....

....

....

....

....

....

....

....

....

....

....

....

....

....

....

....

....

....

....

....

....

....

....

Today, I am grateful for

Today, I am grateful for

Today, I am grateful for

Today, I am grateful for

....

....

....

....

....

....

....

....

....

....

....

....

....

....

....

....

....

....

....

....

....

....

....

....

Today, I am grateful for

....

....

....

....

....

....

....

....

....

....

....

....

....

....

....

....

....

....

....

....

....

....

....

....

Today, I am grateful for

....

....

....

....

....

....

....

....

....

....

....

....

....

....

....

....

....

....

....

....

....

....

....

....

Today, I am grateful for

Today, I am grateful for

Today, I am grateful for

Today, I am grateful for

Today, I am grateful for

Today, I am grateful for

....

....

....

....

....

....

....

....

....

....

....

....

....

....

....

....

....

....

....

....

....

....

....

....

Today, I am grateful for

Today, I am grateful for

....

....

....

....

....

....

....

....

....

....

....

....

....

....

....

....

....

....

....

....

....

....

....

....

Today, I am grateful for

....

....

....

....

....

....

....

....

....

....

....

....

....

....

....

....

....

....

....

....

....

....

....

....

Today, I am grateful for

Today, I am grateful for

Today, I am grateful for

....

....

....

....

....

....

....

....

....

....

....

....

....

....

....

....

....

....

....

....

....

....

....

....

Today, I am grateful for

Today, I am grateful for

....

....

....

....

....

....

....

....

....

....

....

....

....

....

....

....

....

....

....

....

....

....

....

....

Today, I am grateful for

Today, I am grateful for

....

....

....

....

....

....

....

....

....

....

....

....

....

....

....

....

....

....

....

....

....

....

....

....

Today, I am grateful for

Today, I am grateful for

....

....

....

....

....

....

....

....

....

....

....

....

....

....

....

....

....

....

....

....

....

....

....

....

Today, I am grateful for

Today, I am grateful for

....

....

....

....

....

....

....

....

....

....

....

....

....

....

....

....

....

....

....

....

....

....

....

....

Today, I am grateful for

Today, I am grateful for

Today, I am grateful for

Today, I am grateful for

Today, I am grateful for

....

....

....

....

....

....

....

....

....

....

....

....

....

....

....

....

....

....

....

....

....

....

....

....

Today, I am grateful for

Today, I am grateful for

Today, I am grateful for

....

....

....

....

....

....

....

....

....

....

....

....

....

....

....

....

....

....

....

....

....

....

....

....

Today, I am grateful for

Today, I am grateful for

Today, I am grateful for

....

....

....

....

....

....

....

....

....

....

....

....

....

....

....

....

....

....

....

....

....

....

....

Today, I am grateful for

Today, I am grateful for

Today, I am grateful for

....

....

....

....

....

....

....

....

....

....

....

....

....

....

....

....

....

....

....

....

....

....

....

....

Today, I am grateful for

....

....

....

....

....

....

....

....

....

....

....

....

....

....

....

....

....

....

....

....

....

....

....

....

Today, I am grateful for

Today, I am grateful for

Today, I am grateful for

....

....

....

....

....

....

....

....

....

....

....

....

....

....

....

....

....

....

....

....

....

....

....

....

Today, I am grateful for

Today, I am grateful for

Today, I am grateful for

GWY35Q8EZ3

Today, I am grateful for

☼♥☼♥☼♥☼♥☼♥☼♥☼♥☼